The Inner Circle | Henry Bell

Published in 2022 by Stewed Rhubarb
9 Anderson Terrace, Tarland
Aberdeenshire, AB34 4YH

www.stewedrhubarb.org

© Henry Bell 2022

The moral right of Henry Bell to be
identified as author of this work has been asserted.

Printed & Bound by Imprint Digital, UK

ISBN: 978-1-910416-20-4

'Thoughts on Keir Street' was first published in *The Glad Rag*, 'Morning Goodbye off Albert Drive' in *The Interpreter's House*, 'We Were Being Good' in *SoGo Magazine*, 'Comrade Teacake' in *The Dark Horse* and 'Greater and Lesser Winter' in *Cafe Review*.

Stewed Rhubarb gives grateful thanks to Charlie Roy (Head of Publishing Programme), Beth Cochrane (commissioning), Eddie Gibbons (typesetting), and William Letford (editing) for their work towards the publication of this pamphlet.

Brand New * 5

Thoughts on Keir Street * 6

Morning Goodbye off Albert Drive * 8

The Flat Above the Butchers on Maxwell Rd * 9

We Were Being Good * 10

O Watermelons! * 12

The Only Shirt I Iron * 14

Butcher's Boy * 15

Spotlight at The Glasgow Pavilion * 16

Rat Caught in a Manhole Cover * 18

Thi Seccont Burnin * 19

The Gorbals Late * 22

The Smell of the Bus * 24

Tenement Spring * 26

How to Salute a Magpie * 27

Comrade Teacake * 28

Greater and Lesser Winter * 30

Aw Above Themsels * 31

Brand New

Ahinkivrycuntsjistgonnaegitoanwieachother.

        It's gonnae be

                brand new.

Cunt? And what do you mean by cunt?

Ach, it's jist lik me cawin ye yer honour,

                      yer honour.

It disnae mean a fuckin hing.

Thoughts on Keir Street

The smell of rotting lamb in the bins is barely noticeable eventually

The smell of apples and mangoes, decaying or not, is always nice

When a tenement burns to the ground, they'll send a cop to rest outside it for a few months

Cardboard boxes vanish in a downpour but leave a thick grey sludge that hangs about for ages

Wee girls in headscarves playing with toy guns look cool
but it might be bigoted to think so

Some people cook all through every day

When it is clear, truly clear and dry, the sky pulsates right out from the sandstone

Mice are fine when you only have a couple

When it is colder than ten degrees in your flat buying slippers will make you happier than putting cash on the gas will

A drunk man will still call the shopkeeper 'hajji'
'bottle of Buckfast please hajji'

Roma children going through your bins won't hang about
if you offer them food

People don't necessarily believe what they say they believe

It is hard to really sustain a relationship with a neighbour
when water's always pouring from your flat into his

Some people sit and watch nothing all day

Boys love shooting fireworks at each other

No one can go all the way home

You can live on four or five streets, and if you don't leave for a week
you can pretend that there's nothing else out there

If you buy vegetables that you don't recognise you should ask
how to cook them
don't guess

Morning Goodbye off Albert Drive

I'm home half cut
as you get up

keys graze the lock
fingers rucked

on the storm doors' lips
as you open them up

I slur and laugh
you ask the fuck

am I doing soaked
and clearly still up

you're off to work
and I'm in luck

there's eggs in the pan
and tea in a cup

I say 'I love you'
and you say 'yup'

I say I'll cook dinner
when I get up

you kiss my forehead
I wish you luck

St Bert's bells ring
and I hiccough

The Flat Above the Butchers on Maxwell Rd

Rain comes
    through the flashing
drips shape
    stalagmite banisters
it has poured
    long enough to give life
to a chandelier of moss
    and trees
growing out the guttering
    jungle gargoyles
against the Glasgow sky
    rain comes
to run riot down the painted close
    and out the door to the pavement
where the butcher
    chucks his bucket of blood
and sweeps
    the water and the birds away

We Were Being Good

Or A Wanker Came on at Merkland Street

So I get on a train full of Rangers fans,
and I'm reading a book about the Easter Rising,
and I'm feeling a wee bit self-conscious.

Then these six Celtic lads get on at Govan,
steaming.
Can of Dragon Soop each.
Everyone's shouting.
The driver comes back to see what the trouble is.

They all say they're having fun,
and no one wants any bother.
And the driver's like, 'keep it that way lads.'
But of course, the second the train sets off,
everyone's up on their feet,
singing, and banging the walls of the carriage:

'Zombies,' 'Big Jock knew,'
you know the score.

And I'm sat there trying to read,
learning about branches of the Irish Brotherhood
in pre-World War One Glasgow,
and thinking about how football is the worst,

Then, as we're pulling into Partick,
this old boy, covered in union jacks
walks the length of the carriage,

all the way up to the Bhoys' end.
And he stands there,
blocking them in,
chest puffed out,
and he says:

'Fair play tae ye lads, sjist a gemme
an wir aw the same unerneath, aye.'

And then he shakes each one of their hands.

And at that moment, as we're stopped at Partick,
and this old man
is patting one of the young Celtic lads on the back,

right then,

a guy in a Rangers scarf steps on to the train and spits
square in the face of a boy in a green tracksuit.

The man in the scarf jumps off the train,
the train doors shut,
and the boy wipes the yellow spit that's dripping
down his face and says:

'But we were being good.'

O Watermelons!

O honey mango shop!
O slick of sun tan lotion!
ripe back lane bins
and the laburnum's yellow ropes
of poison thrill then fade
so breathe in deep
the back court smoke
a jungle of weed
and bar-b-ques
O buzzing copter!
O row of hot glass bottles!
radios roar from shimmering cars
twins hold
their shrieking guinea pigs
as the Bengal cat
prowls through knee high
yellow thistles
a paddling pool is filled
a phone rings
and a siren ripples
out along the street
O pizza boxes!
O boy racers!

there is a dry heat
that bounces
from sun to tarmac
to sandstone
all around you
till the small relief
of sweat slides down
your face and soaks
into your shirt
O honey mango shop!
O ripe Southside June!

The Only Shirt I Iron

for Sara and Tickle

The Only Shirt I Iron
is on its way
to Govan Old Kirk again.
I have twisted it up,
emptied the pocket of confetti,
and wrung out a christening.
I have hung it up on the pulley
pressed the news into it,
and laid it out for a funeral.
It has sung, and gathered
and shared the smell of the subway,
warm and newly stale.

Today it is at your wedding,
outside this viking cathedral,
standing before a minister
as the Clyde rushes on its way
from the Nile to the Lagan,
stopping only to soak up
a little tonic wine and joy
in the graveyard.

Butcher's Boy

Swipes and skooshes of pig's
blood in my hair. Like I've lost
a fight. Blood caking black
under my nails by the last
stop. Sweat cleans my forehead
carving little paths bordered red and brown.

Inside the van it's dark and cold. I lie
up against the whole hogs stacked
under the refrigeration unit and feel
their cold skin hard and smooth
against my arms and back. I know
the tattooed yellow flesh, the van, is not a spa
but it could be. We stop,

doors swing open and the heat pours
in over me and the meat. I close
my eyes for one last second then jump
down, drag a pig across my shoulder
Hand inside its ribs. Arm against its legs
The pig condenses in the heat, clammy
cold skin and too dry air as I stumble,
try and catch breath, quickly
throw the pig onto the counter,
feet inwards, the weight
needs to be furthest from me,
quick have some small talk ready
for whoever's at the grill.
'Ach no, it's not heavy
It's just awkward.'

Spotlight at The Glasgow Pavilion

Life's a loop of costume changes, jokes and songs: a hologram
Layered truths that, when dissected, become too harsh to understand
But still each part of life refracted is the whole
And watching Annie twice a day is better than the dole

1

Get-in with the stage door open
and rain howling. Stage left: full winter
'thi flairin gaes in thi dookit!'
wet velvet seats, sticky paint and splinters,
and the low barking of a bald stage manager,
everywhere yelling and drookit.

2

                        A break,
the crew room all betting slips, lynx, sweat
microwave meals and ancient jaffa cakes.
Pretend to be on facebook on your phone
or worry at the lip of a roll of gaffa tape.
You can't pronounce anybody's names,
you think one of your colleagues is called Bawbaw.
Another might be Glaiket James.
His girlfriend is definitely called Pocahontas,
you know because she has a name tag
and works at the front desk.

3

                        A bell tolls
twenty minutes before doors open, you dress
in black, then climb the stairs and hide
in a small dark box. Like a lacquered shed
suspended above the Gods.
Warm the light
                  but cover the lens.
Don't spoil the magic. Run through
apertures, check the filter and hingwybob.

4

Scan the crowd for drinkers. Radio down
if you spot bottles opened
                    or better still a hand job.
Headset on: 'aw fuck it's that shite wean
that's Annie the day. And her maw's in.'

5

After the matinee and evening's done,
you climb, light headed, down.
you missed a cue, and didn't light the dog again.
Who cares. You're on the subway home.

Rat Caught in a Manhole Cover

Rat caught in a manhole cover
you have rolled a natural one.
Too fat but not quite greasy enough
you are suspended between the sewer
and the stars: easy prey for dogs, cats
or motorbikes. Dear rat
I do not offer you pity but fellow-feeling,
how rat-like, how human, to dream
of an open road, but find yourself
chained to your dankness.
I bet the other rats make fun of you.
Here, have this poem, it is about your courage,
your hope, your triumph, the way we see you,
full gut stuck in a manhole, straining
and all round the world say 'aah
that brave rat is me.'

Thi Seccont Burnin

Glesca burns bricht
an quick

*Cheapside, James Watt, Elgin Place,
Albert Cross, the Mack*

aw thae heavy metals
dreepin ontae thi pavie
aw thi wid
reevin an malafoustert
aw thon art nouveau delichts
mankit

*Man: sorry tae hear aboot the fire at yer pub Jim
Jim: fuck up, that's next week*

high-rises
swallaed hale by thi soil
Glesca blisters and blinters
hard tae look at it direct
withoot takkin embers
thi size o fists
in yer een
ay it jinks an jouks
an rains hellfire
doon oan Sauchiehall Street
an ootby

ah Glasgow, a tinderbox city
lighting up with each recession

else ither times
its sleekit
oily
skitin past black
lik thi Clyde
eatin itsel
lik an oyster
fu o clart

proud, if anything,
of all that damp ash

Richt noo
a hunner firefighters
are drawin black watter fae thi river
up oan tae thi Glesca Schuil o Airt
where it fries
oan thi bricklin stane
an meltin windaes

followed by a second plague
rats fleeing now full sewers

Glesca burns bricht
an quick
makin itsel new
shootin oanwarts
wi aw that smoke ahint it
an thare
silhouettit
thon Glesca fighters
mixin twa unmellable naitures
Clyde an fire
workin hard
makin somehing

The Gorbals Late

The concrete towers have been clawed back
down to the pavement.
Spires are the only rhythm
as we walk home
from the pub
after the meal,
after the rally,
after the march,
holding hands in happy drunken silence,
counting the way-markers.

Empty kirk, empty chapel, two sets of bones,
the motorway cutting like a cormorant
describing its landing curve
then standing over the Clyde,
spreading its wings, drying itself in the moonlight,
shaking off the slick of the water.

There's a lock-in at the Laurieston
and every passing car
is headed for suburban comfort,
a Marks and Spencer's away from here.

Everyone is missing
from the half-empty strip
of derelict synagogues,
quiet African cafes
and shuttered sheesha bars,
closed railway stations,
filled-in canals.

Till a man in a beard and tarboosh
staggers out into the lamplight,
two children on his back
shrieking with laughter.

We walk past and
catch the gleaming eyes of the father
and the embroidered mirrors of his hat.
They see us struggling to marshal
a trade union banner through the night,
like a roll of red curtain
around our five grinning faces:
a small light
in the Gorbals late.

The Smell of the Bus

The smell of the bus
is strong and specific
a boiled egg is being rolled
along the plastic covered seat

its shell cracks and a man
climbs out
we are passing the city farm
at Tollcross but no one stops

the bus vibrates at the lights
and the newly hatched
man stretches himself, wrapping
his face around a handrail

he pulls at his dough features
struggling for torque on the Strathclyde
Partnership for Transport
chrome he's

making himself a size proper
for a man on a bus he is naked
and fashions a loincloth
from two crumpled Metros

as we approach the centre
the man from the egg rings the bell
and alights where the East End
meets the town

he has taken his opportunity as
we turn a corner and I collect
the pieces of eggshell and place
them in my bag and mouth

Tenement Spring

The last rotten apple shrugged off its snowy hat and fell
three weeks ago and now all at once there are leaves
the gooseberry is a thick fur the raspberries are lanky and wild
everything is cold and wet and green
and the neighbours are outside digging
Maria knocks on the door to collect a parcel
and we smile like it's the very first message to make it through
her wee boy is pulling at her arm
desperate to get outside and end this adult chat
to see the things that are young
and green and new

How to Salute a Magpie
For EM

Find him in his study. Anniesland. Sit. And take his hand.
Trace lovely lines, a photo of Gagarin and an atom bomb,
        all futures good or ungood at rest beneath his beak.

He is a scrapbook bird, feathered, thumbed and fingered,
rearranged to be reread at 90, wings wild wide, and tired.
        As you smile, salute. See Mr Magpie, still a boy

in this fantastic city. Magpie pastes a strong man in,
tastes sweat and tar of workies out on Nithsdale Rd, at the tip
        each finger rips a photo, to be set: a nest of men

and Mayakovsky, riddles thigh deep, arms and lines
cut with precision. Look him in his magpie eye, hope
        he fancies you a bit. Wait for the glint of Poet, pyot

chattermag. This is no nest you've come upon but
a world in full. Hello Mr Magpie, thank you for the multiverse
        the scrapbook, Glasgow, nest, let's spread some glue.

Comrade Teacake

I am watching
a Tunnock's tea cake
fall to earth
in real time
from a height
of 37,262 metres.
It spins and glints. Little
Glasgow Sputnik,
pudding of whimsy,
facing the vastness,
the coldness,
the darkness.
There is nothing better
to do right now
than watch a tea cake
hurtle through space,
115 Eiffel towers above us,
556 Wallace monuments above us,
here in the future.
O little teacake,
from Glasgow to Saturn,
so alone up there.
But imagine
what we will achieve
when you have come back
to earth
sweet cosmonaut.

Your red foil and stars
bring tears
to a kulak's eye.
No empire biscuit this, no.
A teacake
of internationalism,
circling the earth,
spreading
its mallowy joy.

Greater and Lesser Winter

Summer must be taken seriously
in Glasgow where limbs hang out of windows
thrilled to be as bright as the sun

That full ripe Glasgow sun
warming up the courgettes and smashed TVs
beneath the wide sky in my back court

The sky black to my left
bright blue to my right – rains against itself
and the drops dry on the warm concrete

Summer must be taken seriously
when it comes short and sharp
and fills your mouth with the taste of rain

Aw Above Themsels

AhmthatsickaelookinatGovan,
    cannae even be annoyed wi it.
        Ah get oan the subway jist tae get away.

            Ach me tae. And tae get mah veg.
            Ye cannae get fresh veg in Govan.
            No really fresh.

        It's a sin,
    haein tae cross the river for wer messages.
Fur dug food even!
Cannae get the dug food mah Jack likes in,
    no in Govan onymare.

        Well, that's how ah'm gettin a wee cooncil flat in Partick.
        'Whits she daein gettin a cooncil flat in Partick'
          they'll aw be sayin it, oh aye,
        aebdy in Govan'll be that jealous.

        Och no
Rather you than me hen. Ah cannae thole Pertick at aw,
    the erse ae The West End.
        They students, the gentry-ficayshun,
        aebdy aw above themsels.
            Ah'm no for leavin Govan.
Ah'll jist hae the subway fir a wee break.

Acknowledgements

Huge thanks are due to: Liz Lochhead, Juana Adcock, Beth Frieden, Ewan Downie, Calum Rodger and Robin Davis; to the Scottish Book Trust and Jen Hadfield for all their support and wisdom; and to Shane Johnstone for his notes on the poems and on Pollokshields.

And endless thanks always to Livi, Maili, and Frances.